From Boardrooms to Baby Teeth

A Professional Mom's Life Lessons

Tammy Wellbrock,
MS, IOM, CAE

From Boardrooms to Baby Teeth

© 2022 Tammy Wellbrock

All rights reserved. No part of this book may be reproduced except for brief quotations in critical reviews or articles), disseminated or utilized in any form or by any means, electronic or mechanical, including photocopying, recording, or in any information storage and retrieval system, or the internet/world wide web without written permission form the author.

For more information,
please contact the author at:
tammy@tammywellbrock.com

Published in association with Girl Twin Solutions, LLC

Editor: Butterfield Editorial Services
Cover Design by: Scott Gross, 144 DesignCo

ISBN 979-8-9859373-0-5 (Paperback)

Library of Congress Control Number: 2022906253

Tammy Wellbrock

This book is dedicated to
my son, Garrett.

The best gift that I ever got.

From Boardrooms to Baby Teeth

Introduction

I have journaled most of my life, but for ten solid years, I blogged about my many roles as wife, mother, working professional, and leader. While many life experiences inspired me, my greatest muse was my son, Garrett. As his mother, I hope I guided him to be a compassionate, wise, and loving human. In return, he taught me many lessons that I captured within this book to share with others.

My hope for anyone reading this book is that you find as much enlightenment, entertainment, and enjoyment I have had raising this young man! May this book be a tribute to all parents and children who are simply doing the best they can to make this world a better place, with a special hug for those balancing the complexities of working, volunteering, and caring for aging parents like I did.

Unfortunately, my parental journey didn't begin easily. For years, my husband and I struggled to conceive a child. While it is hard enough to accept these circumstances on normal days, the holidays and their child-centered focus really made the festive season less joyful. In fact, I grew to dread the Christmas season and the well-intended questions of our "baby plans." (God bless those people who assume all childless couples are making this choice because they want to focus on careers - that isn't always the case.)

When I finally did get pregnant, we were obviously ecstatic. My due date was projected for early January, leaving us worried my husband would not be home due to his job as a sports broadcaster for our local university. Since miracles have a tendency of surprising us, we were blessed with a healthy baby two days after Christmas. No basketball games or busy schedules to worry about for future birthdays. Now every year during the holidays, I'm reminded of my own answered prayer by getting the best Christmas gift ever.

We were never able to have another child, experiencing one early miscarriage when our son was five years old. Having only one child, my husband and I have tried to be less "helicopter parents" hovering around our child at all times and more of what I like to call "parachute parents" - the kind of parents who provide support from afar, helping him safely land at his destination. Sometimes we were successful and other times, we simply did what we thought was best in the moment. The older I get, the more I realize the only way one knows she has done a decent job parenting is to be able to look backwards when your kid is a grown adult. In turn, the only true way to fail is to simply stop trying.

My motivation in authoring this book was twofold: I wanted to create a memoir for my son, so he understands the impact he has had on this over-achieving mother. Secondly, I hope others can learn (and be entertained!) by my story to become better versions of themselves.

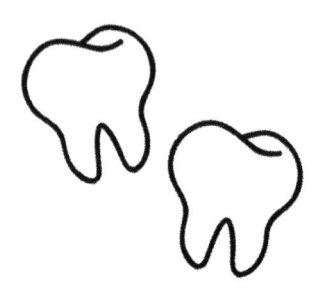

Tammy Wellbrock

When Garrett was only a few days old, he inspired me to write this poem in his honor. It has been the foundation of my parenting philosophy ever since.

This mother's prayer at my son's birth:

Dear little one,
These are my hopes, prayers and wishes for you as we begin this journey together.
- *May you approach every day with a smile and have the rest of the world smile back.*
- *May you show kindness, compassion, and empathy with the many people who pass throughout your life, and that they, too, share the same with you.*
- *May your love of learning be constant, and may your educational opportunities be abundant.*
- *May you continue to stay curious about the world around you, so that you will always be amazed at the wonders which surround you.*
- *May you possess great confidence in who you are and what you do, while remaining humble.*
- *May Guardian Angels protect you, above, below, all around and inside and out.*

I love you to the moon and back,
Mom

Happy reading!

Memory Lane
June 19, 2010 – age 6

Run, Garrett! Run!

When you run, you remind me of the cartoon character Dash, from the movie "The Incredibles." You swing your arms tightly as your legs kick as fast as possible. For as much energy as you exert, you don't propel yourself forward much! Instead, there is a flurry of activity without much progress.

Our advice to you is to make longer strides, so you move in a forward motion at a faster pace. It seems simple enough, but you are having a tough time breaking this habit; you "feel" you run faster with shorter, choppier actions...you think the harder you work, the more successful you will be.

I give you this advice to apply to your future employment. While working hard is admirable, working smart is always more effective, efficient, and successful. Sometimes, by working smarter, you may find an easier way to accomplish the same task. Yet as easy as this is to understand or say, I observe myself and others working in a harder, slower manner. Just because we "have always done it that way," doesn't mean it is always the best way to proceed.

Tammy Wellbrock

Table of Contents

INTRODUCTION

THE "WORK-LIFE BALANCE" MYTH 13
LIFE'S LITTLE LESSONS 221
RELATIONSHIPS 31
PARENTING 355
FUTURE CAREER 41
CONCLUSION 497

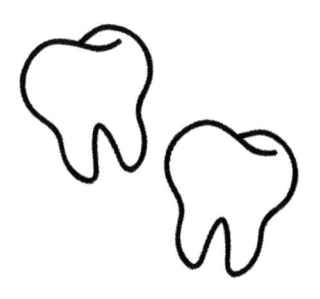

Memory Lane
April 12, 2016 – age 12

Puppy Love

As I completed my nightly routine, I heard you singing from your darkened room. I recognized the new Meghan Trainor song as your young melodic voice drifted through our quiet home: "I'm gonna love you; like I'm gonna lose you..."

Something about the mood was so sweet and melancholy - I just had to make my way into your room to give you another good-night hug.

Tucked under covers and snuggled in each other's embrace was a boy and his dog. I realized the tenderness I heard was the sound of pure emotion as you serenaded your beloved pet. As I bent down to kiss you on your forehead (and earned a lick I wasn't quite prepared for from a certain canine), you whispered to me how you told Buddy you wouldn't have each other forever, so you had to show your love to him every day.

Just when I think I can't love you anymore, you do something to prove me wrong.

CHAPTER ONE:

The "work-life balance" myth

There was a time when my tween-age son was having a melt-down, over what he thought was some terrible parenting decision on my part. In the heat of the moment, he claimed I didn't love him so I did the only thing I could think of to prove him wrong. Opening my jewelry box, I pulled out a handful of small baby teeth and placed them in front of him. I replied, "If I don't love you, then why did I keep these?"

Not only did the gesture stun him into silence, but it also made me wonder...why <u>did</u> I save these teeth? I suppose it is because many moms save everything that measures life-altering moments, from first-step pictures to first-grade drawings. Throughout my home, mementos and treasures overflow from physical folders to digital documents. Yet even today, when I open that same jewelry box and see those little white chompers, my heart still smiles.

Yes, moms do crazy things, like keep painted clay globs of who-knows-what ("It's a crab leg, Mom.") to hundreds of pencil scribblings because we might scrap that perfect album someday. What I have found though, is my son really doesn't care about these grand gestures, but he loves the small aspects I often overlook. Do you know that huge

Thanksgiving feast we slave in the kitchen for days so we can create holiday perfection? Yup, my son's favorite tradition is eating cold ham sandwiches on white bread later that evening. To him, a simple meal wraps up a day spent with family, playing games, and creating memories. I've learned to put less focus on the grandiose and more on simply being present – messy floors and all!

Embrace this:

Stop spending so much time on taking, printing, scrapping, organizing, or posting the picture and just enjoy the moment. It is difficult to find a work-life balance when our focus is fully on what matters most. I learned my son doesn't remember the perfectly trimmed Christmas tree, but he does remember the fun times decorating it together.

When I think about "work-life" balance, I relate this concept to when Garrett was learning to ride a bicycle: he wobbled back and forth, gaining balance along with his confidence. This is so fitting for moms who struggle balancing professional careers with family; balancing relaxation with exercise; balancing fun with play. I certainly don't have the secret formula for surviving the scheduling challenges, but I am learning to give myself a lot more grace and flexibility. Just like the little boy who excitedly threw his hands into the air to celebrate his first venture without training wheels (yes, while still riding), we moms will crash and burn trying to balance all our obligations.

Making the Time

Despite hectic schedules that absorbed many of our evenings and weekend times, my husband and I worked hard at offering as much stability and quality time for Garrett as we could. Doing so often meant we sacrificed our own interests and hobbies. Activities like golf with the men or girl shopping trips were replaced with family game night.

One Christmas, Garrett received the game "Sorry!" We had quite a lot of bonding around that board game. Nothing brought more glee to the eyes of a six-year-old child than sliding down a stretch, knocking out Mom or Dad's pawn. Except sending one of us back to our home base! (And how is it that he always picked up the 'sorry' card right when I was about to enter the safety zone?!?!?!)

We discovered we could turn these experiences into learning opportunities where Garrett could focus on his counting, reading, and strategizing abilities. In addition to learning rules of the games, he learned important life lessons such as being a good sport, win or lose. Over time, the game board has changed, and the time spent discussing what happened at recess evolved into more mature conversations. Don't get me wrong, getting a teenager to open up and talk to parents is a challenge, but positive habits created early on have helped us greatly.

Memory Lane
Nov. 24, 2010 – age 6

Nightmare on 18th Street

The heavy damp vine hugged the side of my body, its leafy tentacles wrapping around first my waist, then my legs. Heat radiated everywhere as I quickly became drenched in sweat. The weight was suffocating as panic began to race through my veins and I...

...woke up to find you snuggled in tight with your arms and legs entwined around me. Your hot sweaty body hugged me full-length as you slept so peacefully. A whole queen-sized bed and the two of us are taking up only a small space. I love to snuggle, but I'd rather not wear my child for my pajamas. No wonder I wake up feeling tired! I think it's time for a nap!

Tammy Wellbrock

Working Full Time

My mom did not work, staying home to raise me and my two siblings. Thirty years later, my husband and I didn't have the finances to afford to live on only one salary. Plus, I had always taken immense pride in my career and work accomplishments. Once, my mom questioned me about my decision to work and I responded with "I work to have health insurance for my family." Regardless, I lived with lots of guilt and mental anguish wondering if my life decisions were in the best interest and well-being of my son.

My mom guilt overtook me one morning dropping off Garrett at my sister's daycare when he was about one-and-a-half-years old. At the time, I was managing a team of twenty employees in four communities, and I was overwhelmed. The supervisory position was intense, as was dealing with upset customers daily. Garrett would not always sleep through the night, so I started each day drained and exhausted. (While driving to one community, I almost drove off the road in a sleepy haze. My affair with coffee began shortly thereafter!) For whatever reason on this specific day, Garrett was extremely upset, clinging to me as I tried to pull away to leave.

I arrived at work with the image of him crying at the front door seared into my brain (I can still picture his teary face years later). I lost it. At work. I called my supervisor and cried. And cried some more. She helped me seek counseling, where they diagnosed me with post-partum depression. The culmination of infertility drugs, hormonal imbalances, new baby, and increased work responsibilities was just too much.

This was a dark time for me, and I still struggle with anxiety and depression today – despite the many blessings I have in my life. However, this journey has helped make me more empathetic, as well as help me make stronger connections with other women who struggle for their own unique reasons. These challenges are not unique to us working moms but for anyone who simply has numerous responsibilities and expectations.

My employment has changed through the years, and Garrett has witnessed my transformation through these positions. Each transition brought new challenges, leadership, and opportunities. These experiences provided me with the entrepreneurial motivation to create my own business. Through training and coaching, I provide tools for women to help them "get out of our own way" so they can embrace their true selves on the search for success. I would not be the resilient woman I am today if not for surviving the tough times.

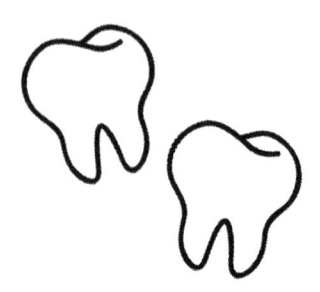

Memory Lane

Mar. 15, 2010 – age 6

Did you miss your blanket?

Having been gone for several days, Dad enjoyed some snuggle time with you, while reading a few books before bedtime. You two caught up on your visit as well, with you asking Dad what he did at the hotel when he traveled for work. In your own way of relating and understanding, you asked Dad, "Did you miss your blanket?" Your own blanket goes everywhere: the couch, the basement, all hotels, grandparents' houses, long car rides. A night without your treasured cloth is difficult, if not, impossible.

Dad reassured you that he was glad to be home with us, as well as to sleep in his own bed. After Dad shared this story with me, I found myself pondering on the bigger meaning of the blanket - how an item can become more symbolic and meaningful than its actual worth. To you, this blanket provides more than just warmth from the chill; it gives you security in the dark, comfort in the unknown, and reassurance when alone. While I may have outgrown the need for a "blankie," I still need a source of strength to get me through life's challenging moments. Missing a blanket can be hard, but not having a blanket at all would be even harder.

From Boardrooms to Baby Teeth

CHAPTER TWO:
Life's Little Lessons

One of the best self-help resources all people should read is "Green Eggs and Ham," written by the wise doctor, Dr. Seuss. This realization came to me as I sat in Garrett's kindergarten class during reading time. In all my experiences with this literature, I narrowly viewed it as a book encouraging children of all ages to try and be open to new things and ideas.

Yet, while balancing my tush on a way-too-small-for-me chair, a new reality struck me. Is this book not the ultimate motivational tool? Sam-I-am never gives up even though he faces hostility as well as excuse after excuse. Sam also doesn't respond emotionally or internalize all the negativity around him. Instead, he keeps exploring new possibilities in his effort to open the eyes of a stubborn and not-so-willing person. In the end, Sam's perseverance pays off. Say, I do like Dr. Seuss, I do!

A notable example of when my son showed perseverance was the entire summer (yes, this was a multi-month effort) he tried to blow a bubble with his bubblegum. With one simple action, Garrett took another step closer to adulthood and becoming the man he is destined to become. I guess one could say I found a higher meaning to chewing gum, so let me explain the correlation between blowing bubbles and maturity.

As a small child, Garrett was fascinated with how people older than him could successfully blow bubbles with their gum, but he could not. This made him feel inferior, young, and incapable. So, after many - many - attempts, he finally taught himself to blow a bubble. (I think I might have strained my neck, turning quickly numerous times to observe a spit-blob hanging from a mouth after a little boy would grunt or whine excitedly to get my attention.)

What I observed was my son experiencing success after failure. He didn't give up on his goal, he continued to believe in his abilities to triumph. I never realized how important small victories can be, but life lessons are all about perspective, aren't they?

Embrace this:

Celebrate the small moments because an adult cannot measure the importance these have on a child's developmental foundation.

For children, these achievements are profound moments and provide the foundation for future learning and personal growth. As adults, we dismiss the importance of minor moments. I'm so grateful my son helped remind me I have as much to learn from him as he does from me.

Tammy Wellbrock

Learning from Failure

When Garrett was in junior high school, I gave him a unique gift. This gift was not wrapped in pretty paper, or even something for which he had asked. In fact, I hadn't planned to give him anything nor did I particularly enjoy giving on my part but give I did.

I gave him the gift to fail. Yes, fail...make a mistake...go down in flames...whatever you want to call it. While singing solo the national anthem at our local university's basketball game, I completely blanked out on the words. I don't even think I made it to the second stanza when...nothing. So, in front of several thousand fans, I stopped, turned around, and asked the announcer to join me in singing. Somehow, I kept my composure, finished the impromptu duet, walked to my seat, and remained glued there for the rest of the game, all while fighting the urge to crawl under the bleachers and hide out until the coliseum's lights turned dark and I could sneak away.

I'm not proud of my very public mess-up, especially since I have sung the anthem perfectly dozens of other times. But I lived through it, and someday, I will try my luck at singing it again. Because I want Garrett to see me live my own advice: to keep trying even when I am scared, unsure, or lacking in confidence. I want my son to know I am proud of him, no matter his mistakes, because he tried when so many others didn't have the courage to take that first step.

Unfortunately, what I want and what I do are not always in tandem. Sometimes, a loving, caring, and supportive parent can make mistakes. In my case, I make many of them. However, I made Garrett feel insecure during his first traveling basketball tournament and for that, I felt like the worst parent ever. Ugh.

Garrett was a third grader, playing his first real game. I admit, I was discouraged to watch him look so lost, overwhelmed, and awkward on the court. While the other boys were hustling and energetic, Garrett appeared rooted to the floor. (I know, he was only eight years old - don't make me feel worse than I already feel.)

Between games, I came up with this crazy idea to offer money to Garrett for each foul he made. My hope was I would encourage him to be more aggressive while letting him know a foul is better than not trying at all. A short while later, Garrett proclaimed to his friends he knew who the worst player on the team was. He answered it was him because "Mom is paying me money to foul out of the game so other better players could play."

Ouch. Score one for the bad Mom.

Instead of a motivational speech, all Garrett heard was "Mom doesn't think I'm good."

His reaction was an uncomfortable mirror reflecting my ugly side. I got caught up in my own ego and desire for my child to be perfect. I forgot the most important rule of all: love my son for who he is and not for what he does. I completely understand no one likes to fail. What I had hoped to teach Garrett is to not let the fear of failure keep him from attempting something new or risky.

Fast forward a few years, and Garrett is a fourteen-year-old sitting for his driver's exam to earn his learner's permit. After encouraging (okay, more like nagging) him for a month to study for this test, he exploded and told me to stop pressuring him.

Whoa, Nelly! After thirty-plus years of driving myself, I forgot how nervous I was at his age to begin driving. I then remembered watching my twin brother take the test immediately after we became of age, but I chose to wait until after Driver's Ed that following fall.

— Embrace this: —

We adults take for granted the experiences our children find daunting or scary. It's good to remember we aren't experiencing life at the same speed. Patience, support, encouragement, and understanding are important skills to have as a parent and as a leader.

When Garrett finally walked into the license office days after his fourteenth birthday, he was a nervous, anxious boy. And when he walked out, he was devastated. Failing at anything can have that impact. He failed his first attempt at the driving test.

Even as adults in the professional world, we intellectually know that failure will happen. When it does, we know we will learn from it and have the potential to grow to be stronger, smarter, faster, better. But dang, it can sure sting when it happens. Like in many life stories, this experience ended well, thankfully, with Garrett passing on his second try.

Memory Lane
Nov. 18, 2011 – age 7

Just Another Day in Paradise

"Mommy!" " MOMMY!"

I woke up mid-stride as I ran toward your room last night, confused and bewildered by the entire situation. The next sounds I heard seeped into my consciousness, forcing me to stop at the hallway closet to look for our "puke bucket." (Surely others also have a designated bowl for such a purpose?)

Alas, I'm too late, and end up catching the volcanic eruption with your comforter. After a quick clean up, I see you have already fallen back to sleep, only to "erupt" an hour later. This time, pillows, sheets, and jammies all need washed. As Dad takes over the linen duties, I take over the child duties.

With a freshly cleaned and changed child, we snuggle into my bed to catch a few more winks. As you drift back to sleep, you ask me, "Do I need to go to school tomorrow?" My answer pleased you as you wiggled closer into my embrace.

Nope, I thought, you just stay right where you are.

Tammy Wellbrock

Profound Thoughts

When people state they loved the "baby stage" or the "toddler years" of their children's lives, I can't help but think that my favorite stage with my son is whichever one he is in at the time. I have taken boundless joy in each of his life phases, appreciating the fact his health allows him to mature naturally as a growing child should.

Besides being in the 95th percentile for his head circumference (I have the C-Section scar to prove this), Garrett has also been above-average with his language skills.

Here are cute examples of him at an early age exploring his language understanding.

#1: While playing with a new toy on my work desk, Garrett struggled trying to achieve the toy's objective. He claimed: "This game is UN-possible!"

#2: As we drove past our local Walgreen's, he noticed the sign stating "1-Hour Photo." He asked what that meant, so I did my best at explaining. After considering my answer, he said he didn't think he would use this service. Baffled, I asked him why not? He replied, "Because it would take five hours to make five pictures!"

#3: Any time Garrett went through a growing spurt, five minutes after every meal, he was hungry again. Before heading to school one morning, we had just put on our coats when Garrett announced he was hungry. Unfortunately, in the last-minute rush, I didn't have any healthy options to quickly offer, so I agreed to letting him eat a small chocolate candy bar. On our drive to school, I explained that the candy bar was not a healthy choice, sharing our family history with overweight struggles. After I told him eating junk food makes us gain weight, he asked "Don't we just poop it out?" (Oh, how I wish!)

#4: Garrett loved to hear about "the good 'ole days" and so I relived when he was a baby still in my tummy. He asked all sorts of questions, like: "When did we go to the hospital?" "Did it hurt?" I didn't share all the details, but I did share how my tummy would roll back and forth when he moved around inside. After listening with an expression of mixed fascination and horror, he declared, "I'm glad I'm a boy."

#5: While driving to school, a voice from a seven-year-old Garrett piped up from the back seat "When I turn Dad's age (he was forty-three at the time), the year will be 2046." Math not being my best talent, I thought aloud, "Let's see, if your dad was thirty-six when you were born, and you are seven now, then that means thirty-six plus 2010 equals 2046. Yep, you're right!" After I marveled at how brilliant Garrett was at figuring out a complex math problem, he told me all he did was add 2003 (the year he was born) to forty-three, to get 2046. Lesson learned: the role of mom is filled with many "duh" moments!

#6: Garrett loves to hear about "the good 'ole days" and for his seventh birthday, I relived my pregnancy experience. He asked all sorts of questions, like: "When did you go to the hospital? Did it hurt? Were you scared?" I didn't share all the details, but I did share how my tummy would roll back and forth when he moved around inside. After listening with an expression of mixed fascination and horror, he solemnly declared, "I'm glad I'm a boy."

#7: Garrett has always had such an interesting way of looking at life. I'm so impressed with his observation skills, whether now as a young man in college or the little boy who informed me that he knew whether a man was going #1 or #2 (yes, talking toilet time here) simply by looking at the direction his feet were facing under the stall doors. His frank observation stunned me in two ways. First, I was amazed at his spatial perception and ability to "look" at life from another point of view. Second, he simplified a routine process in a creative and concise manner. Granted, I am writing about how people go potty, but one needs to look past the topic and see patterns and trends. It's rare for adults to be able to step outside themselves and evaluate or dissect honestly. Maybe it's because he is brilliant (like me), or perhaps children simply have less mental clutter to get in the way of the bigger picture. Either way, he has always been able to teach me in his innocent, direct and wise way.

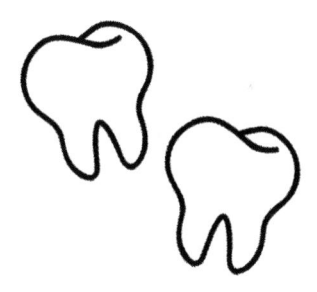

Memory Lane

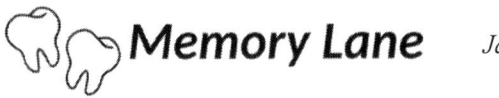

Jan. 17, 2012 – age 8

Child Labor

As an eight-year-old you have a job. And you don't like it. Or so you tell us.

Before anyone cries foul and calls the police, let me explain the "job" at hand. You are now taking piano lessons (I'm sure you would beg others to call the police now.)

For fifteen minutes every day (unless I'm feeling particularly ornery and set the timer to twenty), you are required to practice the piano. Your loving parents gently remind you when you begin to complain, all of us have a job around the house. Your job is to practice the piano.

When I wonder why I added this battle into our daily routine, I remember the important skills you are learning from this experience: self-discipline, goal setting, persistence, time management, as well as music appreciation. It's wonderful to see your self-pride when you complete a song perfectly.

Sometimes, making a child do something "bad" is the best thing a parent can do.

CHAPTER THREE:

Relationships

There is an old adage that I hear often, being the mother of a son: When you have a daughter, you have her for life. When you have a son, you have him until he takes a wife.

A major decision many people make is choosing the right mate to grow old with together. As a love-sick teenager, I remember asking my own mom whether my dad swept her off her feet romantically. I was crushed to hear that he didn't, yet her answer stuck with me for decades: my dad made her heart smile just thinking about him. At the end of every workday, she couldn't wait to see him again.

With every crush, date or girlfriend Garrett has had, this ditty hauntingly floats through my mind. When Garrett was age eight, we celebrated a friends' wedding, with a dance ending the festivities. As the mother and groom danced together, we watched from the sidelines, me rubbing my only child's shoulders. I couldn't help but think that will be us someday. Swaying to the music, I wondered what we would visit about as all eyes are on us. I wondered what I will really be thinking and feeling deep inside. Will I like my future daughter-in-law? Will she like me? What will I think about the woman who will steal's my son's heart away from mine, the woman who will know him better than I ever hope? Will

Garrett become more of a stranger, or will I gain the daughter I never had?

Thankfully, I found a life partner who makes my heart smile as well. Having a solid friendship with my husband has carried us through life's challenges. If Garrett decides to marry, I pray he marries his best friend; someone who makes him happy and helps him be a better human.

Embrace this:

Respect is a simple word that holds power and provides the foundation to which all relationships are formed. Whereas love is something a person feels, respect is the way a person treats another. Yes, I love my husband, but it is because of my respect for him and our relationship that I treat him kindly, considerately, and compassionately. I may or may not like coworkers, but I must respect their opinions and their right to be heard, acknowledged, and treated fairly.

When two people who have a strong partnership start a family, the experience is more profound.

Since fate chose me to have only one child, my husband and I tried our best to provide Garrett with the most enriching life possible. Without siblings to lean on, he often looked to us to serve the roles as confidants or punching bags. While we may not have heard the pitter-patter of lots of feet in our house, we did get to share special times that those in big families do not.

Innocent Love

A tradition my small family had that will always remain special is what we dubbed our "Tri-Kiss." When Garrett was little, he sometimes needed to hop on a bed or chair to get to our level, but then all three of us would lean in for a kiss, forming a triangle with our bodies. Teenage years morphed this into a "Tri-Hug," but I love how the three of us created our own unique way of providing comfort, love, and support to each other.

Perhaps the greatest parenting tool we had to help Garrett become more loving, compassionate, caring, and empathetic was adding a furry brother to the family. When Garrett was in first grade, we rescued a dog from the local pound. Buddy was a mix blend of boxer and terrier, and the bond those two brothers had was instantaneous.

An amazingly astute and sensitive dog, Buddy has supported Garrett through sickness and in health, loving his boy through many of life's demanding times. This dog intuitively knew when to snuggle in during a chilly night or to lick the tears during heartbreak.

I know Buddy was pivotal when Garrett came home one Friday in first grade announcing his best friend "broke up with him." As I understand from his recount, Garrett chose to play basketball alone during recess, rather than playing with his friend, which thus caused the part of the friend-no-more.

Come Monday morning, Garrett worried himself to the point of a tummy ache, thinking that other kids in his class would "break up with me and then I won't have any friends." We were all relieved to find this didn't hold true, and no more break-ups took place, until years later anyway.

While this was an early age to start this kind of peer pressure, I was proud that Garrett stood firm in his desire to do his own thing, despite the "then I won't be your friend anymore" threat. I asked him how he responded when his friend shared this threat; he said, "I told him, 'Fine.'" Learning how to stand his ground then gave him the courage and skills to keep doing so later when the pressure became greater.

— Embrace this: —

Parenting is one of life's rare experiences where you don't fully know if you "did it right" until you can look at the adult child and see a capable, well-adjusted human being.

Maybe a pup helped my son find his inner strength, but I admire how Garrett has learned how to balance self-confidence with humbleness. I've learned much from this young man and believe I am also a better person because of his influence.

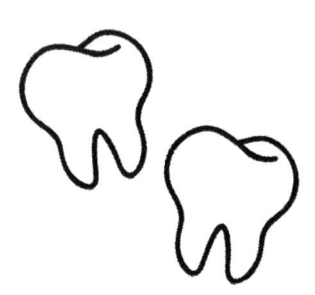

CHAPTER FOUR:

Parenting

I never imagined as a parent I would tell my child things such as:

"Don't lick the TV!"
"Stop licking the public bathroom wall!"
"Did you just lick the trashcan? What on earth would make you lick the trashcan?"

Thankfully, Garrett's need to sample the world with his sense of taste was a passing phase. Parenting is filled with so many rites of passage, big and small measurements of progress that shape childhood experiences while leaving permanent marks on the hearts of mothers and fathers. Whether it was learning how to crawl, losing that last baby tooth, or kissing the first girl, each step paved the way to the next milestone. From my perspective, I was both sad and glad to say goodbye to the Tooth Fairy, Easter Bunny, and Santa Claus, mainly because Garrett was an extremely light sleeper!

— *Embrace this:* —

Having lived our own childhood through a mix of rites, both good and bad, we parents struggle reliving the negative moments again with our children. Hopefully, we won't endure the same challenges. Overcoming our own triggers and not living vicariously through our kids can be harder than one ever imagines.

Rites of Passage

Perhaps the most hilarious rite of passage was the time Garrett threatened to run away because of his mean parents. (Oh, the humanity!)

He threatened to leave often, but only once actually packed a bag and headed out the door. His plan was to stay with his Aunt Pam's family who lived several blocks away from us. While Garrett packed, my husband told him he would not be able to go to as many college games, since his aunt didn't have season tickets. Since they would now have one more mouth to feed with him moving in, he should not expect many trips to McDonalds, either.

The comments didn't stop Garrett and his angry determination on one particular evening; he responded saying we were the worst parents in the world. Reality hit, however, when Garrett stepped out onto our porch. Maybe it was the cold dark night that made him pause, or perhaps it was when his father told him "Goodbye" and closed the front door. After a few minutes, we turned on the porch light, opened the door, and in entered a milder child. I guess we weren't so bad after all.

Memory Lane

Nov. 22, 2012 – age 8

One Thanksgiving, you provided this list of all for which you were thankful…

"My mom, because she keeps me energized and healthy.

My dad, because he gets us free basketball and football tickets.

My grandparents, because they are really nice, and I want to keep them healthy.

My cousins, because they are really fun to play with.

My dog, Buddy, because he is my first dog, and he plays with me and it's really fun.

My friends, because I like them, and I like it when they can come to my house and play."

After you finished sharing, you turned and asked me: "Are those good because's?" (I know that isn't a real word, but I'm quoting here.)

I was struck by your innocence and sincerity. You were trying so hard to convey what fills your heart, but you don't always know how to verbalize your emotions or intentions. Your responses may have seemed simple to us (should I say, jaded?) adults, but to you, those reasons mean the world.

I told you with a smile and a kiss: "Yes, Garrett, those are great because's."

Tammy Wellbrock

Anger Control

From the moment he made his entrance into this world, Garrett possessed an intensity that fueled his anger. Only weeks old, he would get so mad when he couldn't get his thumb into his mouth to suck. On the rare occasion he was successful, he would excitedly wave his arms, starting the process all over. As a toddler, anytime he felt he "lost" a competition (getting dressed last, being shorter, or having only lost one tooth compared to his peers), he would melt down into a pile of destroyed mush and tears.

To funnel these emotions and competitive spirit into a healthier focus, we created the family motto: Try Hard and Have Fun. Whether before school music concerts, youth travelling sports, spelling bees, or high school tournaments, we would recite our motto to try to reduce the internal pressure Garrett placed upon himself.

Raising an intense young child who demands so much from himself requires great parental patience through anger tantrums and crying fits. We also recognized a need for better communication because we realized Garrett simply didn't know how to release his inner turmoil through language, which accounted for behavior that wasn't appropriate and down-right embarrassing! (I have to add though, the time he hatefully told me he was going to "tear up my grocery list" during one of his tantrums still makes me laugh today!)

To help Garrett communicate more effectively while connecting his emotions to behavior, we officially launched the "Most Important Moment." All we asked was for Garrett to think about his day and share one thing that he felt was most important. This later evolved into an after-school routine that involved asking him to share answers to these questions:

What made you happy today?
What made you sad?
What made you laugh?

We would continue asking questions using other emotions, helping Garrett connect with his feelings and situations. He usually couldn't remember what he ate at school and a general question like "How was your day?" received a short "fine" answer, so this routine created good habits that we still use today.

─── *Embrace this:* ───

Parenting for the tougher teenage challenges start when children are babies. Create strong, healthy habits of communication, insight and courage that will provide a solid foundation on which a child can grow.

The most profound lesson I learned regarding connecting with Garrett is when he is ready to talk, I drop everything to listen. As he grew older, the times he was talkative became rarer, and he was most open and vulnerable right before bedtime.

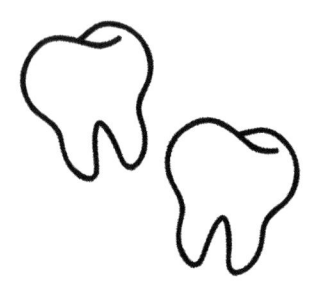

Memory Lane

Nov. 4, 2009 – age 5

Like A Sad, Sad Country Song

Parenting is like a Kenny Roger's song: you've gotta know when to hold 'em; know when to scold 'em; know when to walk away; and know when to put them to bed!

Tonight, you were one tired little boy, who started crying at eight p.m. just because I told you it was bedtime. As we prepared for bed, you cried about this and cried about that. Somewhere in your sobbing rant, I hear you tell me, "And I'm not going to brush my teeth! And those are real threats!"

As we snuggle in bed, you continue crying, telling me how we "never take me to away football games and we are going next week to Missouri." As you segue into wanting to go with me and my friend to Oklahoma, you end your tirade with "and I'm dumb!"

I don't think you thought my response of "Really? I thought you were stupid" was all that funny because your next statement was "And I'm skipping school tomorrow!" How else could I respond to this? Of course, I told you, "But you have to go to school. Remember? Your dumb."

Yup, tonight was definitely a hold 'em night.

CHAPTER FIVE:
Future Career

My husband is a professional sports broadcaster. He wanted to pursue this career as a young boy and so has our son. Like his father, Garrett is passionate (interested, obsessed...) about whatever sport is in season. Not only does Garrett enjoy playing ball, but he also loves recreating plays. (We saw many "silent" fights between umps and managers, as well as slow motion replays of great catches). His impressive-for-his-age observations skills included noticing slight changes in baseball cap design to how the catcher wears his helmet (with or without a cap) to whether the catcher rips off his mask to catch a pop fly.

Early into the beginning of first grade, Garrett came home telling us how the kids at recess played football on Harman Field. Unaware of such a field, we asked him for more details and discovered that he named grassy areas around the playground after the school's office staff (from the principal to the secretary). Let's just say, I've heard similar stories about my husband's childhood as well.

It seems like yesterday I was focusing my camera on the base ready to capture my son sliding head-first while playing T-ball. We have moved on to witnessing him signing to play collegiate baseball to majoring in sports broadcasting; it is exciting to see Garrett truly living his own childhood dream.

Tammy Wellbrock

Memory Lane

Jan. 20, 2016 – age 12

Garrett's version of "in a minute..."

Mom: *It's time to brush your teeth.*
Son: *I will at halftime.*

Unfortunately, for those atypical chats between a mom and her sports-obsessed, child-of-a-sports-broadcaster son, that conversation takes a slightly different turn.

Because in our home, you spend hours playing, calling, or enacting imaginary games with imaginary players, and you keep ongoing imaginary stats for these imaginary teams. The imagination continues with a full schedule, brackets, and post-season. And all these games have coaches' interviews, pre- and post-game analysis, time-outs, media time-outs, rain delays, power outages, injuries...ugh.

So, when I ask you to brush your teeth and you reply "at halftime" this really means nothing to me. It indicates no particular time frame, nor does it mean teeth will actually get brushed.

Don't even get me started on the answer "after the game." You just cannot imagine the number of overtimes one imaginary game can have. Especially when it is close to bedtime.

Kindergarten Equals College

Not only did Garrett give formal names to his elementary school's "athletic fields" (otherwise known as grassy areas), but we also discovered that Garrett imaginatively turned the community's elementary schools into a pretend collegiate system, developing an intricate bracket of imaginary games and rosters between his and the other schools in the "league." Most of the public schools already had mascots, but the private Catholic school did not, so Garrett took care of this task: he dubbed the boys team as the Holy Family Jesus' and the girls' team as (yep, you guessed it) the Holy Family Mary's.

Not only did he remember all the statistics and ranking for each school, but he also recalled the best players' individual standings. This was an impressive feat since these "games" were all played out in his mind and enacted somewhere in our house. This quiet child at school would take one step into our house after school and morph into mode with his "announcer" voice piped up calling a pretend game. Once Garrett received a PlayStation console, we had to distinguish between imaginary games as "fake games" versus "PS3 games." Yes, I have seen more of my share of pretend game highlights and slow-motion replays.

Because Garrett has "called" games since he could speak (and probably before this but we didn't know any better), we became slightly immune to this passion (or skill, or obsession, whatever you call it). One day, I remember pulling a young Garrett onto my lap for a quick wiggly snuggle. I asked him what he loved so much about his pretend games. As serious as he could be, he responded, and I quote: "I really like the game itself, but I especially like it when the game gets intense, and the crowd really gets into it." Crowd? What crowd? Does my kid hear voices?

Tammy Wellbrock

Born a Sports Broadcaster

Here is a wrap up of other moments that still linger in my memory and heart:

🦷 While wanting to vacuum where Garrett played in our living room, I told him to move his baseball game so I could sweep. Without missing a beat, he announced in his best radio voice "and now let's break for a fifteen-second station identification."

🦷 Another time during one of his living room baseball games, I turned on the fan only to hear him state "and it got windy on the field."

🦷 On one stormy evening, a thunderclap caused him to run desperately downstairs into our basement. Thinking he may fear the brewing storm, we followed only to find him pulling out a FHSU Tiger blanket onto the floor. Yup, he was covering his pretend baseball field with an imaginary tarp before the "rain" drenched it.

🦷 It took me two consecutive falls to realize why a quarter would keep showing up mysteriously on our living room coffee table. I would pick it up and dump it into our coin jar, just to find another quarter there another day. Garrett finally told me it was for his "coin toss" before his living room football games.

🦷 While most of his school illustrations were lacking due to his impatient nature, one of his creations left no room for confusion. In kindergarten, Garrett brought home an assignment where he filled in the blanks "A good friend always..." and "A good friend never..." Well, he finished his as "A good friend never pitches and hits the batter in the pee-pee." Yep, a big red circle covered the childish stickman batter right in the you-know-where.

🦷 Whatever the sports season, Garrett will play, watch, read and reenact the sport wholeheartedly. He changes his clothes to match the color of his team during March Madness; our back-yard fence serves well for home runs (and sticks for out-of-bounds markers); and nothing is better than going to the university football practice with his dad (unless the team dares to practice in the area he has deemed his part of the field). We have witnessed on many occasions Garrett coming out on the field or court (aka living room) for team introductions, being the coach, drumming in the marching band, singing the national anthem, calling time-outs, and sitting in the locker room or dug out.

🦷 Before games (pretend and otherwise), I have been asked to prop our American flagpole into the sofa cushions and sing the national anthem, while Garrett either crossed his heart (like a fan) or stood with hands behind his back (like a player).

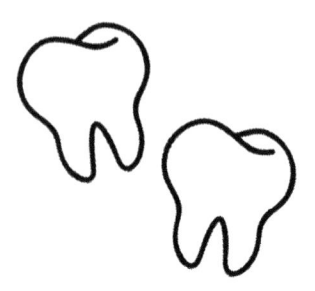

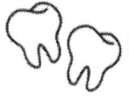

Memory Lane *Dec. 3, 2011 – age 7*

Here was a conversation I overheard with you and your uncle.

"I've got a lot of decisions to make," you said.

"Oh, yeah? Like what kind of decisions?"

"Well, most of my friends know which junior high they will go to, but I'm not sure which one I'll pick because if I go with my friends, I'll probably go one place but if I go with my cousin, I'll go another. Then I'll have to choose a high school, and then I'll have to choose a college."

"What do you want to be when you grow up?" asked your uncle.

"Maybe work at a bank or a restaurant. I'm not really sure because I haven't decided yet."

"Hmmm, that does sound like a lot of decisions to make."

We "grownups" often think about the good 'ole days, when we were kids and didn't have a care in the world. However, kids do have cares and concerns, but most of the time, they simply don't know how to express them. I never would have guessed you were concerned beyond what you wanted for Christmas, but I was wrong. One decision I have made is not to assume I know what you are thinking!

From Boardrooms to Baby Teeth

Conclusion

*J*ust as the year closes to an end, so does this book. Of all the things I've accomplished, being Garrett's mom and watching him grow into an amazing, witty, caring, and wise young man makes me most proud.
(I know this is also true for his dad.)

I compiled this book for his high school graduation, so he would always have at his fingertips a source of love, inspiration, humor, wisdom, and hope for a better tomorrow. It has been fun reliving special memories preparing this collection of stories, but I truly hope this book resonates with all parents who juggle many responsibilities while simply trying to do their best.

Future chapters are yet to be written and now my son takes over the pen, ready to fill in the blanks with a solid foundation to launch him toward new experiences that will continue to shape him along the way.

Thank you for joining me on this treasure chest of beautiful memories so far. Best wishes as you continue to create more on this life journey.

Never forget our family motto: *Try Hard and Have Fun.*

With all my love,
Garrett's Mom

From Boardrooms to Baby Teeth

Author's Note

Women who balances both a career and family deserve a special place in heaven! I think back to when my child was younger, and a sense of exhaustion consumed me!

This book was written more to entertain and support other women rather than provide a handbook on how to survive and conquer this dual role. Since every person is unique, so is the family situation, and my goal was to provide a snapshot into my life so that perhaps another woman would find comfort knowing she is not alone.

Everyone is on their own beautiful and scary journey. While statistics may show numbers of people experiencing infertility, stress, divorce, work pressures, and so on, you still are experiencing the challenge for the first time. These challenges may benefit with counseling is needed, while others may appreciate the coaching experience. Think of a coach as a supportive, yet neutral, thinking partner with whom to share thoughts to find different perspectives or strategies.

It's important for all people to find their support team, whether it be a team created with friends and/or professionals. Simply note that I'm here for you, rooting you on as you continue to do amazing things. It would be an honor to work with you as part of your success journey.

Made in the USA
Middletown, DE
30 March 2023